Henri N

Wounded Healer

William Ruddle

Pastor, St George's St Baptist Church

GROVE BOOKS LIMITED
RIDLEY HALL RD CAMBRIDGE CB3 9HU

Contents

Acknowledgment

Continuing thanks to John Colwell who opened my horizon to Henri Nouwen and to Hilary
Plymen who opened her life in hospitality—a beautiful example of a wounded healer.

The Cover Illustration is by Peter Ashton

First Impression May 2005
ISSN 0262-799X
ISBN 1 85174 593 9

Introduction

I first met Henri Nouwen in the Spring of 1999.

Of course I mean through his writings, for Nouwen himself died in 1996 following a fatal heart attack. As a charismatic evangelical, I approached the work of a homosexual Dutch Catholic Priest with more than a little cynicism. To my surprise, I found in Nouwen a lover of Jesus and a gentle voice calling me to explore with him wounds of insecurity that I had spent years burying. The journey I travelled I would like to share with you now. My prayer is not that you may travel the same path, but that these few pages may whet your appetite to listen to Jesus' calling through the writings of a man I would regard as one of the most significant spiritual writers of the 20th century. In a world, even in a church, that spends so much energy in trying to disregard the scars it bears, we all need to hear the one who calls us to undress our wounds in his presence and experience the healing of Immanuel—God with us.

In this booklet I shall address three central motifs in Nouwen's writing: wounded human;[1] wounded Christ; and wounded healer:

> *Wounded Human*—speaks of us in our fallen, broken state, rushing through life, desperately seeking to deny our inner voice that above all fears aloneness, seeking healing in church, in material things, even in other people, but ultimately remaining unsatisfied and craving something deeper.
>
> *Wounded Christ*—speaks of the Immanuel who emptied himself and became human, allowing himself to be wounded on the cross in order to become the place of healing for all scarred humanity.
>
> *Wounded Healer*—speaks of us as some are called to be, indwellers of Christ who seek to articulate to the world the experience of healing that we have found in his presence, secured through the cross. People who have recognized their wounds, unbound them and dressed them once more—willing at a moment's notice to reveal ourselves in hospitality to others and thus become a source and a place of healing.

Hold these images in your mind; picture them if you can. As we journey into Nouwen's writings, each of these three at different aspects will become clearer, though each is related to the other.

2 The Wounded Human

First, a confession: whilst the other two motifs are commonly found in Nouwen's writings, nowhere does he use the label of 'wounded human.'

I hope he would not have disapproved of it. It certainly helps us avoid much of the language instilled in him through studying psychology that frankly I find confusing.

The concept of wounds is prevalent in his writing and was probably lifted by Nouwen from Carl Jung. Nouwen was not afraid to gather ideas from all spheres, while being heavily influenced by Judeo-Christian spirituality throughout:

> Rabbi Yoshua ben Levi came upon Elijah the prophet while he was standing at the entrance of Rabbi Simeon ben Yohai's cave...He asked Elijah, 'When will the Messiah come?' Elijah replied,
>
> 'Go and ask him yourself.'
>
> 'Where is he?'
>
> 'Sitting at the gates of the city.'
>
> 'How shall I know him?'
>
> 'He is sitting among the poor covered with wounds. The others unbind all their wounds at the same time and then bind them up again. But he unbinds one at a time and binds it up again, saying to himself, "Perhaps I shall be needed: if so I must always be ready so as not to delay for a moment."'[2]

Wounds are an inevitable part of the condition of suffering humanity. Experienced by all, they are ignored by most. As Philip Yancey notes:

> ...much suffering for Nouwen stems from memories, buried deep inside, which release a form of toxin that attacks the centre of one's being. Good memories we display in the form of trophies, diplomas and scrapbooks; other, painful memories remain hidden from view, where they escape healing and cause enduring harm.[3]

This restricts healing as the wound is internalized, and in the solitude of the inner self it develops, festers and grows

Not all suffering results in woundedness, but Nouwen believed that because of the alienation and individualism of contemporary society, many sufferers suffer alone. This restricts healing as the wound is internalized, and in the solitude of the inner self it develops, festers and grows.[4]

Our Key Wounds

But what are our wounds? They have been spoken about in many ways by many voices. Words such as 'alienation,' 'separation,' 'isolation' and 'loneliness' have been used as the names of our wounded condition. Maybe the word 'loneliness' best expresses our immediate experience and therefore most fittingly enables us to understand our brokenness.[5]

Our wounds are not primarily physical but emotional, rarely material but mainly relational. Nouwen lived this understanding, moving from the hierarchical, cerebral atmosphere of a tutoring at Yale University to the L'Arche community of severely handicapped people. Nouwen pastored a group of people who had no hope of finding physical healing nor achieving material gain. Yet Nouwen found healing for himself and others in that close-knit, relational community—he found 'home.'

If loneliness is indeed our central, core wound, experienced universally by humanity, then Nouwen's wounding was particularly severe and deep—one which, were I wishing to critique his writing, he never managed to reconcile within himself. I speak of his abiding aloneness brought about by his homosexual

Nouwen constantly faced challenges to bind up his wound and ignore its effects upon him

orientation. Bound by the constraints of the Catholic Church which he honoured and adored yet being so relational himself, Nouwen constantly faced challenges to bind up his wound and ignore its effects upon him. Should he 'come out' about his sexuality? Should he enter a covert prohibited relationship? Maybe leave the priesthood altogether? He chose none of these. *'Instead, he decided to keep living with the wound. Again and again, he decided.'*[6]

Recognition of Our Wounds as a Gift

Little of this is new. Using different metaphors, the above recognition of the human condition has been spoken about by many before. However, it is Nouwen's appreciation of suffering that is his radical legacy to the world. For most of us, suffering is something to be avoided, grappled with, become victorious over and then left behind. But for Nouwen suffering was 'a deep incision in the surface of our existence which has become an inexhaustible source of beauty and self-understanding.'[7] There is beauty in brokenness. The self-revelation of suffering enables us not only to see within ourselves, but to escape the restrictions of our environs and enter into the common humanity of us all. For we all suffer, all God's children are wounded—we need not be alone. The Christian way of life does not take loneliness away but protects and cherishes it as a precious gift.[8]

> *The Christian way of life does not take loneliness away but protects and cherishes it as a precious gift*

As we enter into our own suffering, we are able to enter into the suffering of others—that is the gift. Many will be reading this booklet because within their faith journey they long to become wounded healers to others. Nouwen's word to us is that in recognizing and bandaging our own wounds we can empathize with the sufferings of our fellow humanity.[9] We can empathize with the suffering of the poor and marginalized in our church, our town, our world.[10]

Speaking with Authority in Our Communities

Who speaks with authority to you? Our institutions of church say the powerful, those in the hierarchies, those who have achieved beyond their contemporaries. (It is present in all branches of the church, though some are more honest in their articulation than others.) My experience tells me that those whom I regard as being authoritative are those who have experienced what I have experienced, those who have walked similar paths before. Nouwen argues that indeed it is only through suffering that we gain authority:

> Those who have entered into human suffering have a special right to be heard. When a widow speaks to a woman who has just lost her husband, she has authority. When a man in a wheelchair gives courage to a boy who has been paralysed by a car accident, he has authority.[11]

Surely this is true. At eighteen, I could not speak with any depth or understanding about tragic bereavement. I had thoughts, even a theology, but I did not have authority. By twenty, having lost a brother to a drug overdose and my father to a fatal asthma attack, I was able to articulate something of worth to those who have experienced sudden bereavement. Surprisingly, such 'sufferings' by God's grace have enabled me to speak to others who may not have experienced the same as me, but who recognize in my story a common thread—an experience of suffering that enables me to embrace them in their pain as one who can empathize, not just sympathize, with their adversities.

Approaching Our Wounds

One may be tempted, in the hope of helping others, to begin carving open one's wounds in public. This needs to be resisted, for you cannot begin the task of unwrapping your wounds unless you are already content in the embrace of God.

> You have to begin to trust that your experience of emptiness is not the final experience, that beyond it is a place where you are being held in love. As long as you do not trust that place beyond your emptiness, you cannot safely re-enter the place of pain.[12]

The place of the rabbi at the gates to the city is not a comfortable place to be and many can recount appalling consequences experienced by those who have sought to lead others when their own self-awareness and contentment in the embrace of God was shallow. We will reflect on this later.

Living with Our Wounds

As I have said, Nouwen believed that all suffering can ultimately be distilled down to the core wound of aloneness. We seek to avoid this through our work, our material possessions and, most frustratingly, through our personal relationships. To counter this flight into relationships Nouwen argues that each of us must heed a call to celibacy, even if we are partnered. We need to recognize that our relationships, however fulfilling, intense and life-affirming, will never make us fully whole. And for any who seek to become wounded healers, we also need to make a space for God to act.

Nouwen argues that each of us must heed a call to celibacy, even if we are partnered

Imagine for one moment your left hand is you and your right hand represents those relationships that are most significant to you. Entwine your fingers. The fingers that reach out to connect are restricted by their connection to the rest of the body. However close and intimate the embrace may be, it is ultimately bound for frustration as neither hand can fully grasp the other. Release your hands and place them in the position for prayer. This is Nouwen's model for healthy relationships—aligned to one another but pointing beyond themselves and moving freely together. Do you notice the almost imperceptible space in-between? That is the inner vacancy, the space in our inner being for God's loving embrace which can be total, fitting and need not ever withdraw.

For us to protect and nurture vacancy for our God in the midst of a society that offers self-fulfilment as our ultimate goal is hardly useful or practical. So let us not be deceived. There is a strong force at work in our world wanting to seduce us. It calls us to believe that standing empty-handed waiting for the Lord is never useful, divesting ourselves of rightful possessions is never practical, and living without an intimate relationship with a companion and without children is certainly never very smart.[13]

Despite Nouwen's inabilities to live this model fully for himself, I find here an insight into the brokenness of humanity that is illuminating. We begin to see the path forward for all who are called to become wounded healers. We may not 'arrive' at our destination in this life, but Nouwen's imperative is, 'Live with your wounds!' Do not see yourself as a wounded woman or man who is incomplete and defective. Instead, lift your eyes to Immanuel, and see in yourself a work of grace undergoing transformation!

Questions

1 What do you find most shocking in this chapter? Why?

2 Which of your wounds are you most apprehensive about unbinding?

3 Reflect upon the requirement to be in a place of contentment with God before undressing your wounds. Does this frustrate you or make sense?

Exercise

1 Re-read the paragraph entitled 'Living with Wounds.'

2 Meditate upon the hand exercises, spending a few minutes in each position, relating where you can to your own relationships with others and with God. Seek the space, the vacancy for God.

The Wounded Christ

3

Our opening chapter was an exercise in introspection.

It encouraged us to consider the fragility of our own lives and happiness. It contained a challenge to recognize the futility of much of what the world and even the church suggests to us as the paths to find well-being and contentment. It concluded with perhaps the most shocking challenge of all — to change our perspectives on our sufferings, to see the potential they contain rather than merely the destruction they have wrought.

In this next chapter we will find the solution, the healer of our wounds. I speak of our second main motif — the wounded Christ. We shall see from Nouwen's writings the wounded Messiah. It is an appreciation of how Christ through the incarnation chose the descending lifestyle, making the decision to be found amongst the marginalized, the dispossessed, the suffering poor. This revelation of Christ gives us hope, present and eternal not only for ourselves but also (as we shall see in the final chapter) for those to whom we seek to minister.

Motif of the Wounded Christ

An understanding of the motif of the wounded Christ is key to understanding Nouwen's work. It is perhaps the cornerstone of his entire spirituality. Of course Nouwen was not the first to draw meaning from the suffering Jesus, but his understanding of Jesus' incarnation and atonement on the cross is like the stone plopping into a calm lake rippling out to his psychological understanding of humankind and the healing role of the Christian minister. I think it is this connectedness of psychological, theological, spiritual and pastoral arenas that has won Nouwen so many millions of admirers around the world. Nouwen's 'Suffering Christ' provides a process that starts at the bottom and works its way even further down.

Nouwen's 'Suffering Christ' provides a process that starts at the bottom and works its way even further down

The Downward Lifestyle

In a world that beckons us to become upwardly mobile, Jesus demonstrated his way was to adopt the downward lifestyle. Jesus gave up all that he possessed, his place with God, his honour and glory, and chose to descend to be amongst the poor, marginalized and disposed—and he calls us to do likewise. Nouwen heard this call and responded. He did not just 'talk the talk'; he also 'walked the walk':

> By moving to Daybreak,[14] Nouwen acted out God's pattern of downward mobility. It went against all his instincts, he admitted. Leaving a tenured position at an Ivy League school to settle among a community of the mentally challenged made no sense by any modern measure of success…In fact what others saw as a pattern of downward mobility in his career path, Nouwen himself saw as a form of 'inward mobility.' He withdrew in order to look inward, to learn how to love God and be loved by God so that he could beckon others into that love.[15]

Nouwen was driven by the Jesus he found in the gospels. Our Jesus was to be found not in the high places of life, in the temple, in the Pharisee's home, in the courts—but in the gutter places of life, with those who were disregarded by their society, shunned because of economic or social poverty. It would be remarkable for a wealthy man to live the life of a slave; how much more astonishing it was for God in person to descend in the form of a poor, weak helpless baby, and then go still further into human frailty and woundedness on the cross. This downward path was irresistible for Nouwen.

We must be careful not to think of this as a riches to rags to riches story. God does not work his way up to greatness once more. 'He chose it not once but over and over again. At each critical moment he deliberately sought the way downwards.'[16] The Jesus who was learning and questioning the teachers at twelve years of age stayed in a tiny backwater until

Jesus stayed in a tiny backwater until he was thirty

he was thirty. The Jesus who was without sin chose to align himself with sinners by being baptized in the Jordan. The Jesus who was full of divine power regarded turning stones to bread, seeking popularity and being counted as great in the eyes of the world as temptations.[17] Jesus opted again and again for what was small, hidden and poor.

> The story of our salvation stands radically over and against the philosophy of upward mobility. The great paradox which Scripture reveals to us is that real and total freedom can only be found through downward mobility.[18]

This call to the downward lifestyle may be alarming and disconcerting for many. For the essence of Christianity is to follow Christ, wherever he may go. Jesus calls us downwards to a place where our titles, our education, our security and our abilities are disregarded. Yet Nouwen's comforting word to us all is that in that place we will find one another, we will find Jesus, and in him we will find freedom.

The Poor as Messengers of the Gospel

I ask myself, do I want to go to such a place? Do I want to find that kind of freedom? An honest reflection asks, how can I know that the security I have is worth rejecting for the healing that Jesus offers? The poor are our sign-posts—our messengers of the good news of Jesus:

> Growing up means becoming healthier, stronger, more intelligent, more mature and more productive. Consequently we hide those who do not affirm this myth of progress, such as the elderly, prisoners and the mentally retarded. In our society, we consider the upward move the obvious one and tend to treat the poor cases who cannot keep up with us as sad misfits, people who have deviated from the normal line of progress.[19]

Yet it is their very deviation from the banal (which we call normal) that calls us to look deeper within. It is in the suffering of the poor that we find the strongest challenges to the securities we have built around ourselves. Nouwen realized this when he moved to pastor the L'Arche community at Daybreak. It was at Daybreak that the needs of the community, the woundedness of the community forced him to deal with his own needs, his own wounds.

> Handicapped people are not only poor; they also reveal to us our own poverty. Their primal call is an anguished cry: 'Do you love me?' and 'Why have you forsaken me?' When we are confronted with that cry, so visible in those who have no capacity to hide behind their intellectual defences, we are forced to look at our own terrible loneliness and our own primal cry…Jesus has lived this primal cry with us: 'My God, my God, why have you forsaken me?'

How often when we have visited that sick person in hospital, the bereaved widow at home, the tragically injured, the lonely single mother have we clamoured to leave, thinking if not saying as we depart, 'There but for the grace of God go I'? I recognize that my riches limit my ability to connect with their poverty, yet I ask myself are these simply an obstacle or actually a fortress? If such is true then I misunderstand the good news of Jesus. For Jesus is there with the sick, the bereaved, the injured and the lonely. Jesus has travelled that road before and offers himself to us in the hospital bed, in the wheelchair, during the lonely nights. The poor challenge us in our faux securities and it is in their presence we must find ourselves saying not 'There but for the grace of God go I,' but 'Here, by the grace of God, is my saviour Jesus.'

The Atonement of the Suffering Christ—Our Poor God

Understanding the atonement is almost a contradiction in terms. Yet somehow we need to listen to Nouwen's incomplete thoughts in the hope that in the 'mystery' of the cross, we might begin to understand how all that is promised is effected. For it is at the cross that we find wounds healed and aloneness comforted.

On the road to Emmaus, Jesus walks with Cleopas and his friend in a most intimate way. He tags along, happy to just be where they are and go where they are going.[20] Jesus has already suffered in the tomb. He has experienced the expiration of the body, the ultimate sign of death, the perfect symbol of desperation.[21] Now once again on the road he is ready to say something entirely new about life from death: *the most tragic, the most painful, the most hopeless circumstances can become the way to the liberation you long for most of all.*[22]

As one commentator puts it:

> Nouwen believed then that, in a mysterious way, wounds could become a means towards both hope and healing, just as 1 Peter 2.24 describes the transforming power of the bruises of Christ—'He himself bore our sins in his body on the cross, so that, free from sins, we might live for righteousness; by his wounds you have been healed.'[23]

How can *'hopeless circumstances become the way to the liberation you long for'*? How can Nouwen believe that *'wounds could become a means towards both hope and healing'*? The answer is simply that in our deepest, darkest most painful circumstances , our Calvary moments, where the forsakenness of God seems total and irreversible, we can find solidarity in the poor Immanuel God drawing near to us. On the cross, God does not pretend to lose control in the death of Jesus but actually, genuinely and absolutely empties himself—makes himself poor. At that moment on the cross, Christ is as poor as you or me. He is truly one with us—a friend for the journey:

God does not pretend to lose control in the death of Jesus but genuinely empties himself

> He has been sent not only to console poor people but also to give this consolation as one of them himself...When, finally Jesus is hanging on the cross and cries out with a loud voice, 'My God, my God, why

> have you forsaken me?' only then do we know how far God has gone to show us his love. For it is then that Jesus not only reaches his utmost poverty but also showed God's utmost love.[24]

Of course it would be an incomplete atonement if we saw the total effect of the cross as simply being Christ with us in our suffering. Indeed, by his wounds we are healed—humanity is restored. But Nouwen is beckoning us to see that we are healed *through* our woundedness, *through* our God becoming poor alongside us rather than being healed *from* our woundedness, being taken away *from* our suffering.

Nouwen does not want us merely to make the best of a bad situation but to choose to face suffering. I am not suggesting that Nouwen has a masochistic discipleship in mind! But he does recommend a radically different perspective to the inevitable suffering of life. Do not avoid it, embrace it! Do not skirt around the edges but revel in our oneness with Christ in those moments. Christ models this approach and calls us to do likewise:

> Jesus' attitude to suffering and death was quite different. For him they were realities he encountered with his eyes wide open. Actually, his whole life was a conscious preparation for them. Jesus does not commend suffering and death as desirable things; but he does speak of them as something we ought not to repudiate, avoid or cover up.[25]

A Suffering Perspective for the Church

To find healing *through* our wounds not *from* our wounds is for many of us profoundly disturbing yet instinctively attractive. We find the rhetoric of the supposedly blessed Christian life impossible to reconcile with the realities of our broken, suffering world. We articulate (rightly) the blessing of being in relationship with Jesus while hiding away our woundedness for fear of letting down the gospel message. But we will only ever reconcile these seemingly disparate elements of our faith if we see God and the gospel differently. We need, and God's world needs, the church to have a suffering perspective on its wounded healer, Jesus.

We need to learn from the example of Peter, a faithful and loving friend to Jesus but someone whose vision was all too often at odds with Jesus' own view of his mission. We do not speak of pain and suffering, we ignore and hide those away who do not get a quick-fix, cure-all. We thank God for healing but rarely value those who continue to live faithfully through suffering day after day, living the good news of Immanuel with us. But Jesus' rebuke to Peter is startling, *'Get behind me Satan! You are a stumbling block to me; you do not have in mind the things of God, but the things of men'* (Matthew 16.23).

Peter avoided every opportunity on Good Friday to become part of the story with the suffering Christ. My reading of Jesus' prophecy at Peter's reinstatement after the resurrection is that Peter did finally manage to follow in the way of the cross (John 21.18). We are Christians, we do things the Christ way, which as Nouwen points out leads us to a place where we see suffering and woundedness as an opportunity:

> To look suffering and death straight in the face and to go through them oneself in the hope of a new God-given life: that is the sign of Jesus and of every human being who wishes to lead a spiritual life in imitation of him.[26]

Questions

1 If you sensed an authentic calling to a downward lifestyle, how would this be displayed in your life?

2 Who are the poor in your community? How do they speak to you?

3 In what ways are a poverty stricken God appealing or disturbing for you?

Exercise

Consider times where you may have represented the good news in such a way as to eliminate the suffering church from it. Rehearse how you might speak again of the blessings of faith without negating the reality of suffering.

The Wounded Healer

4

If the wounded human was the problem for Nouwen and the wounded Christ the exemplary solution, then the wounded healer is the grounding of that solution in everyday life.

Undoubtedly the singular motif that Nouwen will be most remembered for is this concept that Nouwen calls us to engage with. Nouwen's wounded healer is a challenge to apply our theology, to put our understanding into practice, to become wounded healers ourselves.

First the context. Nouwen did not conceive his notion of a wounded healer alone. As we have said, some have suggested that he borrowed it from the work of one of his mentors, Carl Jung. Jung challenged the *status quo* of his day in the field of psychiatry when he argued that it is impossible for the doctor to heal her patient from a distance. The doctor/patient relationship must be exactly that, a relationship. If they do not engage in their common humanity then they cannot engage at all:

> As a doctor I constantly have to ask myself what kind of message the patient is bringing me. What does he mean to me? If he means nothing, then I have no point of attack. The doctor is effective only when he himself is affected. Only the wounded physician heals.[27]

The need for the doctor to open him/herself up to his patient, to enter into the space under investigation was deeply attractive to Nouwen and was a central tenet to his healing model of ministry. Lived out through the activity of hospitality, the wounded healer can only be effective when he himself is open to being healed.[28] A symbiotic relationship must be created where a constructive and productive interdependence is acknowledged. Living with the L'Arche community at Daybreak, Toronto crystallized this for Nouwen. Here Nouwen experienced a shared longing, the common woundedness of aloneness, symptomatically different but united at its core. Here at Daybreak, Nouwen learnt to

A symbiotic relationship must be created where a constructive and productive interdependence is acknowledged

receive as well as give, '*there is no longer any distance between the helper and the person being helped.*'[20] Nouwen understood the power that such a relationship could bestow upon all those who were prepared to invest in such a bilateral conversation. As Jung had described decades earlier, '*It often happens that the patient is exactly the right plaster for the doctor's sore spot.*'[32]

So we have a symbiotic relationship built not on hierarchy but on commonality. How are we supposed to become wounded healers? What do we bring to this relationship that stops it simply being two wounded people together? How is healing brought about?

Read again the old legend of the Talmud.

> Rabbi Yoshua ben Levi came upon Elijah the prophet while he was standing at the entrance of Rabbi Simeon ben Yohai's cave...He asked Elijah, 'When will the Messiah come?' Elijah replied,
>
> 'Go and ask him yourself.'
>
> 'Where is he?'
>
> 'Sitting at the gates of the city.'
>
> 'How shall I know him?'
>
> 'He is sitting among the poor covered with wounds. The others unbind all their wounds at the same time and then bind them up again. But he unbinds one at a time and binds it up again, saying to himself, Perhaps I shall be needed: if so I must always be ready so as not to delay for a moment.'[31]

The Messiah was to be found sitting with those who were poor, those who were marginalized and forgotten by society. Nouwen calls us to do likewise if we seek to minister in Christ's name:

> So it is...with the minister. Since it is his task to make visible the first vestiges of liberation for others, he must bind his own wounds carefully in anticipation for the moment when he will be needed. He is called to be the wounded healer, the one who must look after his own wounds, but at the same time be prepared to heal the wounds of others. He is both the wounded minister and the healing minister.[32]

We are called to go and be amongst the poor. Not simply to minister *to* them, but to be *with* them. It is here amongst the poor that we perform key functions that enable us to *be* wounded healers. We are wounded healers who articulate. We are wounded healers who guide. We are wounded healers who witness. Nouwen calls us to recognize and embrace these three functions as we grow in this healing ministry.

Wounded Healer as Articulator

Nouwen believed that at the heart of all our woundedness is the core wound of aloneness (see chapter 2). Clearly any survey of his own life shows it was an issue that ravaged him throughout his ministry. This isolation was exacerbated by a sense of living on the periphery of other people's lives, the minister only being invited in at key moments of crisis and delight (birth, marriage, death) but being sidelined throughout the rest of life.

Those who seek to care for others are called to spend as much time as possible unbinding and binding our wounds with Jesus

It is difficult to know how much of his own woundedness is attributable to mankind universally and how much is a result of his own experience, but Nouwen's central argument is that those who seek to care for others are called to spend as much time as possible unbinding and binding our wounds with Jesus. We do this so that we are then able to articulate to the world something of the source of restoration:

> It is this wound which he is called to bind with more care and attention than others usually do. For a deep understanding of his own pain makes it possible for him to convert his weakness into strength and to offer his own experience as a source of healing to those who are often lost in the darkness of their own misunderstood sufferings.[33]

Just as in the legend of the Talmud, the minister must pay special attention to her wound. Whilst others may wish to ignore their wounds and seek to bandage over their distress with people, careers, relationships that cannot truly satisfy, the minister must embrace her wounds and then articulate that experience to others. The minister unwraps and redresses her wound with great care and contemplation so that she is always ready to get up and go to others lost in their own, particular darkness and say, 'Look, this is my wound. This is how I live with my pain. This is my experience of Jesus, the wounded healer.' Caution must be applied to ensure this does not degenerate into the wounded healer simply offloading her woundedness onto the broken and fragile. The recipient finds healing not simply in the recognition of wounds in others but in being ushered towards Jesus' healing presence.

Today many are left to find healing on their own

This function of the minister as wounded healer is in increasing demand. In a society that is becoming progressively geared towards individuality and away from community there is a growing need for us to articulate something of the suffering common to those we minister to. Whereas there used to be extended family units, faith and social groupings with whom to share this story, today many are left to find healing on their own. People crave someone to articulate something authentic, something that the chat-cum-agony-aunt shows created for TV entertainment simply cannot supply.

We must become articulators of the inner events and so to '*offer others creative ways to communicate with the source of human life.*'[34] We are wounded healers who are willing to speak that which has become uncomfortable to speak. We undress the bandages of others not by force but by acknowledging our own wounds and speaking of how we have found healing. My experience is that church communities can find special value in those who are able to articulate and share their own woundedness and their journey of healing with others.

> Articulation, I believe, is the basis for a spiritual leadership of the future, because only he who is able to articulate his own experience can offer himself to others as a source of clarification. The Christian leader is, therefore, first of all, a man who is willing to put his own articulated faith at the disposal of those who ask his help. In this sense he is a servant of servants, because he is the first to enter the promised but dangerous land, the first to tell those who are afraid what he has seen, heard and touched.[35]

Becoming articulators of life's inner events is not without its obstacles.[36] I have found that some, particularly those whose bandages are bound so tight to pressurize their wound from bursting out, react violently against such honesty. The articulator can be deeply threatening to some, and so we must proceed with caution. Articulators have to live authentically, appropriately exposing warts and all to the world. In doing so, we encourage others to live authentically. We function, 'as an articulate witness of Christ, who puts his own search at the disposal of others.'[37]

Articulators have to live authentically, appropriately exposing warts and all to the world

Wounded Healer as Guide

I think the function of wounded healer as articulator was paramount in Nouwen's mind, but other functions are also worth noting as we seek to minister. Nouwen encourages us to see ourselves (and ideally others to see us too) as guides on this journey into the inner life. Those of us in pastoral ministry share a frustration when we see so many people seeking solace in the wrong places and in inappropriate ways. We are called to try and guide towards what is valuable, towards what is healthy and healing:

> Perhaps the main task of the minister is to prevent people from suffering for the wrong reasons. Many people suffer because of the false suppositions on which they have based their lives. That supposition is that there should be no fear or loneliness, no confusion or doubt. But these sufferings can only be dealt with creatively when they are understood as wounds integral to our human condition. Therefore ministry is a very confronting service.[38]

We are to guide people not away from their pain but into it. We show them how they can find healing living with their woundedness not circumventing it. How radical an idea is this! Rather than trying to find quick and easy exit strategies we invite people to explore their pain more deeply, guiding them on the way. This is no easy task and in my experience is rarely embraced wholeheartedly. Yet Nouwen is right, surely? It is not enough to simply place a bandage over a wound, however all encompassing that bandage may be, if we do not know within ourselves what has brought about that initial discomfort. Such a path is folly, for the infection will simply manifest itself elsewhere at a later date (often in a more dramatic and damaging way than before).

Thus the role of the minister is to be prepared to lead the person into the darkness of their inner being, a place of course the minister is qualified to go because he has visited his own depths and indeed constantly returns there:

> A minister is not a doctor whose primary task is to take away pain. Rather he deepens the pain to a level where it can be shared. When someone comes with his loneliness to the minister, he can only expect that his loneliness will be understood and felt, so that he no longer has to run away from it, but can accept it as an expression of his basic human condition.[39]

This is a refreshingly different approach to the counsel we may offer. The models I studied at seminary were keen to ensure the counsellor did not claim an empathy for the client's pain. Pain was as unique as the individual. Yet Nouwen's model of the wounded healer as guide offers a unity at a deeper level that escapes other counselling models:

> Making one's own wounds a source of healing, therefore, does not call for a sharing of superficial personal pain but for a constant willingness to see one's own pain and suffering as rising from the depth of the human condition which all men share.[40]

This may be better explained in an illustration that Nouwen uses in *Wounded Healer*.[41] He presents the tragic picture of a woman who has lost one of her children. The minister is not called to enter into her sadness and draw her out, reminding her that she still has two healthy children who need her and in whom she can continue to take joy. Instead, he is challenged to help this mother realize that the untimely death of her child is a shocking reminder of her own mortal condition and the frailty of life. Yet in that frailty of mortality she has comrades in those around her, for we all share in this same precarious condition and it is a wound to us all that unites and binds us. I cannot save the mother in pain, but I can draw alongside her, allow my own story of pain and restoration to be a resource to her, articulate my own sense of helplessness and offer to join her in her place of isolation:

I cannot save the mother in pain, but I can draw alongside her

> No minister can save anyone. He can only offer himself as a guide to fearful people. Yet, paradoxically, it is precisely in this guidance that the first signs of hope become visible...When we become aware that we do not have to escape our pains, but that we can mobilize them into a common search for life, those very pains are transformed from expressions of despair into signs of hope.[42]

This notion of the wounded healer as a guide I find quite powerful, compared to the traditional understanding of ministry where I seek to bring a ministry comfort into the lives of those around me. Traditional forms of pastoral ministry have seemed to me to exclude the humanity of the minister from the ministry he or she seeks to bring. I never knew the ministers I grew up under. When I sought help from them, whilst their words may have been wise, they were definitely detached. The problem I was bearing upon entering into dialogue was still mine and mine alone when I left. For my minister to bring himself into the conversation would have been seen as unprofessional at best and maybe even selfish and egotistical. It was a one way street that was offered, never affording the opportunity for the healing to be reciprocal.

The problem I was bearing upon entering into dialogue was still mine and mine alone when I left

Nouwen presents a different model that I find persuasive and more importantly for me, a more comfortable mantle to wear. I have attempted to 'experiment' with this model over the last year or so, often allowing myself to enter into the pain of another, allowing the community I seek to pastor to see the wounds that I bear (when relevant!). This is not to say that I am often talking about my personal circumstances, but that encouraging the other to see the commonality in our wounds is a rewarding experience. If the central direction of the path we are treading is, as Nouwen suggests, loneliness and isolation, then it is remarkable to see how guiding people down the path that I myself am treading has seemed to release the other person to explore their own discomfort in safety. As a wounded guide, I believe my role is to say to the intrepid explorer, 'It is OK, you can tread this path, we are all travelling the same path.'[43] This is how I understand Henri when he said,

> The real spiritual guide is the one who, instead of advising us what to do or to whom to go, offers us a chance to stay alone and take the risk of entering into our own experience. He makes us see that pouring little bits of water on our dry land does not help, but that we will find a living well if we reach deep enough under the surface of our complaints.[44]

Wounded Healer Who Witnesses

The third and final function Nouwen sees for the wounded healer is one of witness. As witness we perform an anchoring role. We testify from our own journey that the wounded healer, the liberator we seek to remove us from our suffering, is actually performing his healing work in the present as well as in the future. We corroborate that he is sitting amongst the poor and broken here and now:

> That is exactly the announcement of the wounded healer: 'The master is coming—not tomorrow, but today, not next year, but this year, not after all our misery is passed, but in the middle of it, not in another place but right here where we are standing.'[45]

As ministers of the gospel of Jesus Christ, the good news of Jesus, we must bear witness to the Christ who is liberating us day by day as he sits with us. The fact that Christ is present with me, bringing about a new creation within me *is* my story. Broken but being healed in the present, rather than awaiting some future glorification is the reality I testify to:

> If indeed we…believe that ministry is a sign of hope, because it makes visible the first rays of light of the coming Messiah, we can make ourselves and others understand that we already carry in us the source of our own search. Thus ministry can indeed be a witness to the living truth that the wound, which causes us to suffer now, will be revealed to us later as the place where God intimated his new creation.[46]

Questions

1 Nouwen invites wounded healers to fulfil three functions—articulator, guide and witness. Which function would challenge you most in your current approach to caring for others?

2 Nouwen invites us to share ourselves with those we seek to care for. How difficult would you find this? What are the potential blessings and potential dangers that you could encounter?

Exercise

Consider forthcoming pastoral encounters. Pick one situation where you feel you may be able to attempt to put this approach into practice (I would suggest something not too traumatic/difficult). Prepare for this encounter by thinking about ways you can appropriately share yourself with the person you meet.

Hospitality: The Gift of the Wounded Healer 5

We have gained an understanding of the problem, the divine solution and the functions that we wounded healers must deliver if we are to minister in the way Nouwen suggests.

But what of the mode of delivery? How do we offer these roles of articulator, guide and witness to those we minister to? A deeper understanding of hospitality is Nouwen's answer.

> How does healing take place? Many words, such as care and compassion, understanding and forgiveness, fellowship and community, have been used for the healing task of the Christian minister. I like to use the word hospitality, not only because it has such deep roots in the Judeo-Christian tradition, but also, and primarily, because it gives us more insight into the nature of response to the human condition of loneliness.[57]

The English language has lost what hospitality is truly about. We see it as surrounding external things such as food, warmth, housing etc. Nouwen calls us to explore the etymology of the word and thus find a mode for ministry.

The German word for hospitality, *gastfreundschaft* means friendship for the guest. The Dutch equivalent, *gastvrijeid* translates freedom for the guest. This is the starting place for everyone who would seek to be a wounded healer—to offer friendship that does not bind and freedom which does not leave alone.[48]

Hospitality may not be comfortable for us, for a paradigm shift occurs in true hospitality away from an ideological battle or a spiritual ladder to a place of equalness together:

> Hospitality, therefore, means primarily the creation of a free space where the stranger can enter and become a friend instead of an enemy. Hospitality is not to change people, but to offer them space where change can take place. It is not to bring men and women over to our side, but to offer freedom not disturbed by dividing lines…It is not a method of making our God and our way into the criteria of happiness, but the opening of an opportunity to find their God and their way.[49]

As wounded healers, we do not 'do.' Instead we need to be present for others. We are still pro-active, but our activity centres around ourselves, creating an atmosphere into which others can enter. Creating that void/space for others to enter into is hard work and we must resist the temptation to fill it. Our most important question as healers is not, 'What should I say or do?' but, 'How do I develop enough inner space into which the story can be received?'[50]

> Healers are hosts who patiently and carefully listen to the story of the suffering strangers. Patients are guests who rediscover their selves by telling their story to the one who offers them a place to stay. In the telling of their stories, strangers befriend not only their hosts but their own past.[51]

This model of ministry has some deeply attractive qualities to it. If both parties enter the relationship with an expectation of finding healing together, the concept of me healing you is vanquished. For those in pastoral ministry that takes considerable amount of their time, the expectation of our communities that we will make them better is unrealistically burdensome and fuels the burnout that so many 'career carers' experience.

> ...it is possible for men and women and obligatory for Christians to offer an open and hospitable space where strangers can cast off their strangeness and become our fellow human beings...that is our vocation: to convert the *hostis* into a *hospes,* the enemy into a guest and to create the free and fearless space where brotherhood and sisterhood can be formed and fully experienced.[52]

Questions

1 How different is Nouwen's understanding of hospitality to your own?

2 What practical steps would you need to take to offer a 'free space' to those who seek your help?

Nagging Questions, Appreciative Conclusions

6

There is much to commend Nouwen's model of the ministry of wounded healers to the world, but three significant questions remain.

The first is his impoverished Christology. Whilst the image of Christ amongst the poor is deeply attractive, it is not balanced by an equal emphasis on Christ risen and ascended. It is not the sacrifice of Christ alone which brings salvation but also his resurrection; in baptism and through faith we are both buried and raised with him. In seeking to find God with us in poverty, therefore, Nouwen may have blurred his vision of Christ in glory.

Though in some unpublished work, Nouwen speaks of Christ's wounds as being part of the glorified body, I wish he had made more of this in his published writings. It is for the reader to decide whether Nouwen separates the glorified Christ too far from the incarnational Christ. Personally I think he just manages to hold the two together, even though he does not do this as clearly as in the book of Revelation, where the one who sits on the throne is the paschal lamb—the sacrificed one.

A second concern is how this model can be mis-applied. John McFarland notes,

> The wounded-healer pastor may become an inward-looking chaplain of the emotions who forgets her or his function as a prophet of God and servant of those in need.[53]

We must heed these words of caution. The difference between the wounded healer sharing her story as a resource for others' benefit and spiritual self-flagellation is one of motive, nuance and subtlety. The one who seeks to minister in this way must be constantly asking questions such as, 'Why am I sharing this? How does this help the other? What are the risks here for our relationship?' Failure to maintain integrity in these relationships is reprehensible and could be very counter-productive.

My third concern, however, is the chasm between the wounded healer model espoused by Nouwen and the torment that ravaged his own life and ministry. This raises questions as to how rigorously his model can stand up to clinical practice. However, on those occasions when I have sought to embrace Nouwen's approach, rather than the more traditional and distanced model, I believe that it has been highly rewarding for all concerned. Many others to whom Nouwen wrote and spoke have also testified to its transformational power.

Perhaps we can see Nouwen's struggle as an unfinished work, which included the struggle to be totally honest about himself to himself and others. This is not to devalue his willingness to share his journey with us, and with a rare degree of humility and psychological insight. Through reflecting on his own experience he was able both to assess the human condition and to restate in a contemporary way the effect of entering into the way of the cross. Nouwen's synthesis of faith and experience offers an immensely valuable map for those searching for a spirituality which will both enable their own growth and allow them to minister effectively to others.

If there are nuggets of truth in what you have read, you will probably have found them in quotations from Nouwen. If you have never picked up one of his books, please make the effort to find one (there are nearly 100 to choose from!). You will find in his writings that familiar, attentive, prayerful presence that literally hundreds of his pen-friends speak of. I, with them, thank God for Henri Nouwen, a wounded healer who in his writings still offers hard-won wisdom for our common journey towards God and one another.

Getting into Nouwen—Further Reading

Michael Ford, *Wounded Prophet* — An excellent overview of the entirety of Nouwen's life.

Henri Nouwen, *Reaching Out* — Explores further the idea of hospitality as a model for ministry.

Henri Nouwen, *Wounded Healer* — The starting point for anyone who seeks to understand Nouwen.

Henri Nouwen, *Letters To Marc About Jesus* — A beautiful and simple insight into the Jesus that inspired his writings.

Notes

1   *NB* Nouwen himself used the term 'Wounded Man' throughout his work, but I have sought to be gender inclusive where possible in this text.

2   Taken from the tractate Sanhedrin as cited in H J M Nouwen, *Wounded Healer* (Darton, Longman and Todd, 4th ed, 1996) p 82.

3   P Yancey, *Soul Survivor* (Hodder and Stoughton, 2001).

4   H J M Nouwen, *Wounded Healer*, p 83.

5   H J M Nouwen, *Wounded Healer*, p 83.

6   P Yancey, *op cit*, p 289.

7   H J M Nouwen, *Wounded Healer*, p 84.

8   M Ford, *Wounded Prophet*, p 57.

9   H J M Nouwen, *Our Greatest Gift*, Part One, chapter 2.

10 H J M Nouwen, 'By The Poor,' *Sojourners* (11: January 1982) pp 17–18.

11 H J M Nouwen, 'The Authority of Suffering,' *Sojourners* (6: November 1977).

12 *ibid*, 'Go Into Your Place of Pain' p 22.

13 H J M Nouwen, *Clowning in Rome*, p 56.

14 A branch of the L'Arche communities of mentally handicapped people near Toronto, Canada.

15 P Yancey, *op cit*, p 298.

16 H J M Nouwen, *Letters to Marc about Jesus*, p 39.

17 Nouwen's phraseology here, *ibid*.

18 H J M Nouwen, *Letters to Marc about Jesus*, p 13.

19 H J M Nouwen, *Letters to Marc about Jesus*, p 13.

20 H J M Nouwen, *Letters to Marc about Jesus*, p 8.

21 'Finding new life through suffering and death: that is the core of the good news. Jesus lived out that liberating way before us and has made it the great sign,' *Letters to Marc about Jesus*, p 25.

22 H J M Nouwen, *Letters to Marc about Jesus*, p 9; for further insight, see M Ford, *Wounded Prophet*, p 57 where upon citing the story of the Talmud, Ford concludes, 'Nouwen explained that Christ had given this story a fuller interpretation and significance by making his own broken body the means to liberation and new life.'

23 M Ford, *Wounded Prophet*, p 63.

24 H J M Nouwen, *Letters to Marc about Jesus*, p 39.

25 H J M Nouwen, *Letters to Marc about Jesus*, p 24.

26 H J M Nouwen, *Letters to Marc about Jesus*, p 26.

27 C G Jung, *Memories, Dream and Reflections* (Fontuna Press, 1963) p 155.

28 We shall come back to the idea of hospitality later in this chapter.

29 J Beumer, Henri Nouwen, *A Restless Seeking for God* (Crossroads Publishing Company, 1997) p 63.

30 C G Jung, *Memories, Dream and Reflections* (Fontuna Press, 1963) p 156.

31 Taken from the tractate Sanhedrin as cited in H J M Nouwen, *Wounded Healer* p 82.

32 H J M Nouwen, *Wounded Healer*, p 82.

33 *Wounded Healer*, p 84.

34 *Wounded Healer*, p 37.

35 *Wounded Healer*, pp 38–39.

36 Of course inner events can often be generated by external influences.

37 *Wounded Healer*, p 99.

38 *Wounded Healer*, p 93.

39 *Wounded Healer*, p 92.

40 *Wounded Healer*, p 82.

41 *Wounded Healer*, p 93.

42 *Wounded Healer*, p 93.

43 I say 'we' because I have found the wider witness of the gathered Christian community to be a real help.

44 *Reaching Out*, p 14.

45 *Wounded Healer*, p 95.

46 *Wounded Healer*, p 96.

47 *Wounded Healer*, p 88.

48 *Reaching Out*, p 48.

49 *Reaching Out*, p 49.

50 *Reaching Out*, p 69 (see also pp 71–75).

51 *Reaching Out*, p 69.

52 *Reaching Out*, p 43.

53 J McFarland, 'The Minister as Narrator,' *The Christian Ministry*, Jan 1987, p 20.